Your Eternal Choice

Your Eternal Choice

PAUL H. DUNN

Bookcraft
Salt Lake City, Utah

Library of Congress Catalog Card Number: 81-69180
ISBN O-88494-438-7

2nd Printing, 1981

Lithographed in the United States of America
PUBLISHERS PRESS
Salt Lake City, Utah

Most wrong choices before and after
marriage are made *not* out of
rebellion or intentional error
but out of misinformation, miscommunication, and lack
of understanding.

In most cases,
if couples truly understood the whats and
hows and whys of eternal marriage,
no one would have to talk them
into the right choices. Indeed,
no one would be able to talk them out of them!

Preface

In our world,
marriage
means vastly different things to different people:
Its meanings range from the one extreme —
where it is a frivolous formality,
dried ink stains on a piece of paper —
to *our* extreme, our LDS extreme,
where it is the most important institution
of time and of eternity.

This is a book about our extreme,
about the full scope of what we believe marriage to be —
about how to prepare for it,
how to make decisions regarding it,
how to start it,
how to preserve it.

This is a book that starts with the questions
we all must ask:
the *why, who, when, what, where* and *how* of marriage.

When the questions are general,
and absolute answers for them exist,
I have tried to present them straightforwardly,
candidly, even starkly.
When the questions are personal,
and answers differ for every individual,
I have tried to give the formula
by which personal answers can be sought
and found
and confirmed.

Most of all, this is a book about
the *joy* of marriage.
God gives us counsel on chastity,
on commitment,
and on other aspects of marriage
for one reason:
He wishes us to discover the greatest joy —
the joy that makes us one with each other,
the joy that makes us one with him,
the joy of eternal marriage.

Acknowledgments

For many years now, Richard Eyre and I have felt that a need existed for a very direct and straightforward book on LDS marriage.

We have taken a "before," "during," and "after" approach, starting with the decisions and preparation that precede marriage, moving then to the meanings and significance of marriage itself, and concluding with the eternally significant patterns set in the first months of a new marriage. Discussion of the manuscript with various friends caused us to add the final section on regenerating and revitalizing marriages that are not so new.

As in past writings, Richard Eyre and I have pooled our thoughts and discovered that the result was larger than the sum of its parts. Several of the thoughts in this book stem from books we have previously co-authored; other ideas come from Richard's books *The Discovery of Joy; What Manner of Man; Simplified Husbandship, Simplified Fathership; Teaching Children Joy;* and his newly published novel *The Awakening.*

We dedicate this book to our wives, Jeanne and Linda, who, of course, are our teachers as well as our fellow students in the eternal school of marriage.

A special thanks to Sharene M. Hansen, my able secretary, for her usual attentiveness to detail and typing.

Paul H. Dunn

Contents

I
The
Right
Preparation

Why?

Why Marriage?

Looking back into eternity
we have always been children,
and there was only one father, and that was God.

Looking ahead into eternity
many will share
the God-like role of *parent*.

The single most significant role-change of eternity,
the transition from child to parent
and from brother-sister to husband-wife,
occurs here in the moment called mortality.
We call the transition
"marriage."

There is nothing more important,
nothing more consequential,
nothing more lasting in potential.

But marriage is more than important.
It is practical,
it is natural,
and it can and should be wonderful.

Benjamin Franklin said,
"A single man is like half of a pair of scissors."
The total sharing, total caring
of marriage
opens up furrows of feeling
we didn't know were there,
brings currents of commitment,
new levels of love,
new journeys of joy.

Within the theology of the restored gospel
we can ask (and answer) a great question
that would be unanswerable elsewhere.
The question is:
"What achievement can qualify us
for the highest form of exaltation?"

The right answer to that question is
the reason and the basis
for this book.
Before we look at the right answer, let's consider
some wrong ones:
financial success;
higher learning, academic degrees;
athletic ability;
fame.

Obviously none of these qualifies us for exaltation.
Let's consider some other achievements:
How about . . .
Church positions,
genuine love of one's fellow men,
personal integrity and righteousness?
Certainly at the end of this list

we're moving into achievements that affect
salvation and exaltation,
but the question
"What achievement qualifies us for the highest
form of exaltation?"
is still unanswered.
Its answer is *eternal marriage.*

Eternal marriage
is the training and testing ground
for genuine love and personal integrity.
It is oneness with each other and with Christ.
It is the opening of God's role to us.
It is the only passport to the highest level
of the highest degree.

Eternal marriage and temple marriage are inter-twined.
Temple marriage is the starting block;
eternal marriage is the finish line.
Temple marriage is an opportunity;
eternal marriage is its fulfillment.
Temple marriage is a ceremony;
eternal marriage is a way of life, a way of love.
Temple marriage is potential;
eternal marriage is promise.
The effort of this book is to offer some assistance
in preparing for the first
and then
in turning it *into* the second.

It would be easy to go on answering the question
Why marriage?
because there are so many answers.
But presumably you know most of them;
that's why you're reading this book.

For Instance:
The Class Reunion

It seemed incredible — ten years since high school graduation. Ben had stayed in touch with some of his friends, but there were others, others whom he'd been very close to that he hadn't seen or heard from in years.

Ben had been married for six years, and he had two children who meant the world to him. His family life with them and with his wife, Amy, was far and away the most fulfilling and happy part of his life. "In fact," he thought, "it *is* my life." For that reason he was particularly anxious to see Dick and Sheldon, two of his closest high school buddies who had never married. Ben had heard from each of them once in a while; their situations were very different from each other. Dick had just "never found the right girl" and claimed still to be enjoying the bachelor's life. He was active in the Church and in the Special Interest program. Sheldon, on the other hand, had apparently taken a stand against marriage. He had left the Church, had lived with a succession of different partners, and had written to Ben that he considered marriage an out-dated institution.

Ben's first impression at the reunion was that neither of his friends had changed that much, at least not in personality. Dick was still quiet and analytical and deeply thoughtful of others. Sheldon was still uninhibited, still made everyone laugh, still commanded the center of attention.

It was only later on, when they had a chance to talk personally and privately with each other, that Ben noticed how they had changed. Dick confided in him: "I feel like I'm spinning my wheels, Ben. I'm earning a good living, I have Church jobs, I have friends, but I'm not really growing. I compare myself with you and our other friends who have families, and you are in a whole different dimension than I am." Ben noticed a longing look in Dick's eyes, almost a hollow look. He noticed that Dick was more nervous than he had remembered him; that his expression hinted a perpetual trace of worry.

But Sheldon was the real concern. After listening for a half-hour to his private descriptions of the joys of the immoral life, Ben looked him straight in the eye and said, "Are you really happy, Shel?" His old friend started a typical answer. "Well, of course I'm happy, Ben. That's what I'm telling you — how happy I am. I've had more pleasure in the last year than you'll have in a lifetime." His voice trailed off as he looked into Ben's eyes. Then he looked away.

When he looked back there was moisture in his eyes. "Oh, well, I never could lie to you, Ben. No, I'm not happy. Oh, I have fun. But each time the fun's over, Ben, I'm lonely; I'm sick inside. No one would believe this, but when I go home alone I either cry myself to sleep or drink myself to sleep. It's the pits!"

Because of the distance between their homes, Ben didn't see Dick or Sheldon again until the fifteen-year class reunion. During the interim, though — and much to Ben's delight — a wedding invitation came from each. If there had been any way, he would have gone to both weddings, Dick's in the Salt Lake Temple and Sheldon's civil ceremony. As it was, the years passed and their next meeting was at the next reunion.

Sometimes complete changes can best be described with simple words. Dick now had a maturity and peace in his face that had been missing before. He had started a family, and he knew the joy of caring for others more than himself. Sheldon was even more drastically changed. His wife, it turned out, was a non-Mormon but a Christian in the deepest sense who had made Sheldon see the value of commitment. Sheldon was still funny, still fun, but in a less selfish way. He seemed more interested in others, less self-centered, and far, far happier. Before the day was over, he pulled Ben aside and said, "You know, Patty's been asking about the Church. I didn't feel worthy to answer her but I *did* know lots of the answers; and as I see how much sense they make to her, they start to make sense again to me. I've got a lot of repenting to do, Ben, but with Patty I can do it. Don't miss the twenty-year reunion, buddy, because we'll have the same kind of marriage you do by then!"

Why Chastity?

Have you ever asked yourself these questions:
Why would God restrict us from some things —
advise us strongly against them?
warn us?
even command us?
Are his commandments just arbitrary whims,
artificial tests of some kind,
generalities that are important for some people
but not for others?

Of course not.
His commandments are
loving counsel from a wise Father.
Our understanding and concept of God
as a loving and personal Heavenly Father
allows no other definition.
He gives us commandments for one reason only:
he loves us and wants us to be happy.
His commandments are our signposts to happiness.
We have the power to discover that for ourselves.
We can break commandments
one by one

and discover that each violation
sooner or later
creates unhappiness.
We have the power to discover that, but not the time.
God, who knows which actions bring joy
and which actions detract from it,
has *told* us
so we don't *have* to experience
the pain of discovering all of them for ourselves.
As we heed the loving counsel of his commandments
we can use our lives instead
in the discovery of joy.

Chastity is the perfect example.
God simply knows
that virtue is its own reward,
that the saving of oneself
for one eternal partner
makes that commitment more beautiful,
more joyful.
It is the simple question of whether you want
a penny now
or a diamond later.
Any momentary pleasure that might result from
pre-marital sex
cannot be compared with the vastly greater joy
of oneness in marriage.
And the indulgence in the former
can destroy the potential for the latter.

Chastity is like money in the bank.
As you save yourself
you are saving
the joy of belonging to one
and only one.

You are saving the joy of being able to say,
"I am all yours
and I have never been anyone else's."

Some will ask,
What if we already know
who "the one" is?
What if the commitment is already there
and we're just waiting for the ceremony?
The answer is that it's not just a ceremony,
it's a covenant—
both with God and with your partner—
and *waiting*
shows the deepest love and respect for both.

Some will say,
"But we love each other too much to wait."
The answer is that
there is no such thing as too much love,
and that it is too much selfishness—
not love—
that debates divine counsel and violates virtue.

Any love that is to become eternal
must include respect, faith, trust, admiration, and
    honor
and must have spiritual and mental aspects
as well as physical and emotional.
No relationship,
either temporal or eternal,
can exist without these attributes.
(Every soap opera is filled
with accurate illustrations of misery brought about
because these qualities are absent.)

If, in your case, the physical tends to dominate,
all the more reason to *bridle* it
and find the other dimensions.
Bridle is the word wise father Alma used
in counseling son Shiblon,
and the promise he attached is the key to
        understanding.
"Bridle all your passions,
that ye may be filled with love."
Bridling increases strength, increases power, increases
        love.
There are two ways to absolutely control a horse —
one is to kill it, one is to bridle it.
Alma did not say kill your passions.
The implication is *not* that passions are evil,
that we shouldn't have them.
On the contrary,
we bridle something we love,
something whose power we respect.

A horse is stronger than a man,
so the man bridles it,
thus *controlling* its power and using that power for
        good.
Passions are stronger than we are,
so we bridle them,
thus controlling their power
and using that power to strengthen a marriage
and forge it into eternity.
One has to know *how* to bridle a horse
or a passion.
The following case study will help.

A final word
to summarize:
Sex is simply too beautiful to squander,

too wonderful to waste.
It is the sterling silver
too precious
to tarnish before the beauty of the banquet.

For Instance:
A Decision on Deposit

Kalvin was committed to the Church and to its way of life. One of the most important discussions he ever had took place at dawn one morning while he was in a boat, fishing with his older brother, Ray.

Ray had been married for a couple of years, happily so, and Kalvin used the privacy of the boat to ask Ray some questions about the physical aspects of dating that he had never been able to ask anyone else:

Where do you draw the line?

How do you decide how far to go?

Ray answered with simple wisdom that he later decided must have been inspiration.

"It's not so much knowing what the right decision is, Kal; you already know that. The key is *how* and *when* you make that decision. If you just say, 'Oh, I won't pet, I'll follow the standards of the Church,' you haven't really made a specific and personal decision, and you haven't committed yourself totally to it. If you wait until the moment when you are tempted and then try to decide specifically how far you'll go, you will almost certainly rationalize and go too far."

Ray looked at his brother, saw the trust in his eyes, and went on. "Look, this may embarrass you Kal, but I'm going to describe as vividly as I can a situation you may find yourself in some day, and I want you to tell me just exactly what you would do."

And Ray did. He described Kalvin alone late at night with a girl he liked very much. He described the emotion in the air and the dizzying physical attraction. He described hands that wanted very much to go beyond where they should. Then he asked Kal to describe what he would do.

Kalvin's answer was too quick. "I'd take her home."

"Yes, Kal, but imagine it's actually happening. *Describe* what you would do."

Before the morning was over, Ray had extracted from Kalvin a detailed description of actions — what he would say, how he would reach for the key and start the car, what he would turn the discussion to. He had lived the experience mentally and completed it successfully.

Ray was pleased. "The decision is made now, Kal. You haven't come to the situation yet, but when you do, you'll have the decision with you, already made, ready to use. It's like money in the bank — there when you need it."

Both Ray and Kalvin had pretty much forgotten the discussion in the boat until a year and a half later when they were both at their parents' home during the Christmas holidays. Kalvin pulled Ray aside and said, "Remember our talk in the boat? Well, it happened to me, Ray, just as you described. And I *did* what I described to you — I said what we practiced, I turned on the car, I took her home. As I walked down the steps from her porch, I looked up at the stars and shuddered. I realized —I *knew*—that if I hadn't thought the whole thing through in advance, *in detail*, I'd have done the wrong thing. Thanks, Ray. I love her, and that morning in the boat saved something pretty important — for both of us."

Why Repentance?

Change!
All of the gospel's admonitions
and all of its promises
and even its *purpose*
hang on that word.
The message of Jesus Christ is *change*.
The promise is that we can change —
change our minds,
change our hearts.

Yet many of us inwardly disagree.
We say, "People never really change.
I can't change."
We listen to the light and beauty
of a talk on the rewards and value of virtue
and feel like dark outsiders
looking at the light from far off
but unable to climb into it
because at some regretful moment past
our virtue was lost.

We forget the simplest and most important assurance
of Christ.

Lost virtue can be regained.
All of the Savior's messages —
in fact his very atonement —
center on the reality of repentance
and the fact of forgiveness.
An innocent and well-intended
but deceitfully wrong illustration
has often been used to describe repentance.
It is the nail-in-the-board story:
A sin is the driving in of the nail,
Repentance is the pulling out of the nail —
but the nail hole remains in the board.
Wrong!
Repentance is more analogous to the waves of the sea.
If sins are footprints in the sand,
real repentance removes them exactly as totally
as if they had never been there.

Satan uses every device to thwart repentance
because, when it is true, it beats him every time.
He tells us that the hole will still be in the board;
he tells us the embarrassment of confession is too
        much;
he tells us the sin is too small to worry about,
or else he tells us it is too big to repent of.
Often, he tells us that it is a private matter,
that it should not be confessed
until we have overcome it personally.
What a trap!
By getting us to keep it inside,
he forms a secret combination with us
and keeps us from the relief and release
that come with confession
and from the help that priesthood leaders would give.
By keeping it secret,
he increases his chances of getting it to happen again.

Remember, guilt is God's prompting to confess.
Confession is the method
by which guilt is released.

Repentance is beautiful
because it restores beauty.
None should fear it.
All should be grateful for it.
All should *use* it.

For Instance:
True Forgiveness, True Forgetfulness

Becky had experienced, as a teenager, a true incident of repentance. She had committed a moral infraction and, after deep soul-searching and prayer, had gone both to the Lord and to her bishop with sincere regret and confession. She had also sought forgiveness from the boy with whom the disobedience had occurred.

Hard as the confession to the bishop was, the feeling that resulted was worth it all. It was as though an enormous weight was lifted from her shoulders and was shared with the bishop who, with love and concern, helped her work out the process of repentance. He set up future interviews as checkpoints in the repentance process. Becky followed through and worked hard at her prayers and at the internal changes required. At last, in prayer, she had the welcome feeling of forgiveness.

Time passed. Becky went away to college and met a wonderful returned missionary. They were married in the temple, and they started their family on the east coast where he was attending graduate school. Becky's long-held worries about how he would react to a mistake she had once made seemed silly after she had told him (the night of their engagement) and after he had put his arms around her and wept with her in their trust of each other and their shared belief in repentance.

A year after their marriage, they returned home for a visit and Becky went to her old ward for the first time in several years. Her old bishop was still there, though he was no longer the bishop. Becky felt a sudden rush of gratitude toward him, and she pulled him aside after sacrament meeting to thank him.

The bishop looked at Becky with a trace of confusion in his eyes and said, "Becky, I'm not sure I know what you're thanking me for."

Becky was more specific. "For the time you helped me repent of a moral infraction, bishop. It changed the whole course of my life!"

The bishop looked searchingly into Becky's eyes. Then he said, "Let's take a walk outside for a moment."

As they walked around the block, the bishop held Becky's arm and said, "You know, this has happened to me before. I literally cannot remember your coming to me with a moral problem. I remember you as one of the sweetest, dearest young women we ever had in the ward, and my memory's good on other things, too. But I have decided that the Lord has blessed me with one of his gifts—the ability to completely forget sins which have been set right. That is what he does, Becky. I know that. His promise is that he forgives and forgets. Real repentance makes a thing as though it had not happened."

The bishop turned toward her. "I love you, Becky, and so does your Heavenly Father."

Note: Remember, the Lord's promise is not that *you* will forget the sin, but that *he* will remember it *no more*. While you may continue to recall the incident, the pain of it will pass.

Who?

Who for Eternity?

You may have bought this book specifically
for the answer to this all-important question of whom
   to marry.
Alas,
the book can't give it to you.
But it can (and will) give you the formula
whereby you can discover that answer for yourself.
The question itself is a frightening one —
and it should be.
Whom to spend eternity with,
whom to bring children into the world with,
whom to share everything with forever,
whom, ultimately, to populate worlds with —
how can any mere mortal (especially one of tender
   years)
make a decision like that?
He can't!
He simply can't know enough
or project accurately enough.
Then God must make this decision for us — right?
Wrong!
For is not one of the reasons for mortality

a standing on one's own,
a learning to think, to decide, to act?
So if it's too big a decision for us,
and if our Father won't make it for us,
who does?
Answer: We make it together.
Our best effort is coupled with and protected by
his veto power.
But more on that later.
What about those who don't yet have
a specific decision to make—
the girl who's not been asked,
or the boy who's not been close to asking?
Where are the guarantees that "the right one"
will ever appear on the scene?
Some ask this question too much,
so much that they become preoccupied with it,
and thus too anxious to impress,
too self-conscious,
too impatient in a situation that may take *years*
instead of the days they may have in mind.
The tendency, for some such people,
is to work too hard on the situation
(which is usually beyond their control)
and not hard enough on themselves
(which *is* within their control).

Instead of worrying endlessly
about where he or she is
or about where you should be
or what you should say, or do, or think
in order to find him or her—
start worrying instead about who *you* are
and what you can become
and how you can progress within yourself
while you are waiting for him or her to come along.

Let's assume your highest priority goal is temple
   marriage,
but you know you've not yet found "the one."
Perhaps a subtle change of thought
is in order.
Perhaps your highest priority goal should be
to become a more Christlike person.
(*That's* something you can work on *now* in several
   ways
and something that will prepare you
and qualify you for a better partner
with regard to the other goal.)

For Instance:
The Disciple Decision

Jared had been home from his mission for a year,
and he had recently fallen desperately in love. He was
head over heels. He couldn't keep his mind on anything. He had the world's worst case of spring fever.

Along with the emotion of love, he felt the emotion of
fear. For twenty-two years people had told him how
crucial the marriage decision was. The last thing his
mission president had said to him as he boarded the
plane bound for home was, "Be sure you find the right
one, Elder."

So now he was in love. But was love a guarantee that
this was *it*? How to know? How to decide? Somewhere
in his memory was a scriptural guide to decisions. Who
was it? Where was it? Someone who had tried to decide
something for himself had been chastized . . . Oliver
Cowdery, that's who it was! Now *where*?

Jared found it in the ninth section of the Doctrine &
Covenants: ". . . you must study it out in your mind;
then you must ask me if it be right." (D&C 9:8.) *Seems*

simple enough, thought Jared. Heaven only knew he'd been *thinking* about it enough to qualify.

That night (and time after time in the days and nights that followed) he asked the Lord for a decision. "What shall I do? Is she the right one? Is this thy will?" He phrased it in a hundred different ways.

But no answer — no feeling certain enough to be sure it was not just what he was *wishing* to feel.

Despair! Ecstasy mixed with despair.

Jared acted on impulse. He got into his car and drove a few miles to the bishops home. "I need to see the bishop," he blurted to the bishop's wife at the door.

She looked at his anxious face and smiled, part in surprise, part in amusement (she had seen this look before). She showed him into the living room.

"What can I do for you Jared?" The bishop put out his hand.

"I have a question I can't answer," Jared stammered.

"What is it?"

"It's . . . Well, it's whether I should get married!"

The bishop smiled. "That's easy," he said. "You *should!*"

"What I mean . . . what I mean is — should I marry Lydia."

"Well, now, Jared, that's a more difficult question. Let's talk a little about Lydia."

He asked everything from, "Does she love children?" to "Can she bake a cherry pie?" And Jared was positive in every response.

Then there came a silent moment, the bishop looked searchingly into Jared's eyes. "You've been troubled about getting the Lord's answer haven't you? In fact, you've been troubled by the ninth section."

Jared looked up with a start. He wanted to say, "How did you know?" But instead he said, "Yes, sir. I have studied it out in my mind and asked the Lord for an answer, but none has come."

The bishop sat quietly, listening, and then a slow knowing smile spread across his face. "You have misunderstood the scripture. You have left out the *middle step.* The scripture says, 'If it is right I will cause that your bosom shall burn within you; therefore, you shall feel that it is right.' This is a general promise — for all decisions. If *your decision* is right, he will cause your mind to know it. He will *confirm* your decision for you."

Now the bishop was teaching a principle. He sat back in his chair and went on. "There are three steps, Jared. One is to study it out — thoughtfully, prayerfully — in your own mind. Two is to make *your own* best decision. After all, learning to think and decide and be agents to ourselves is one of the *reasons* for mortality. Three is to *take that decision* to the Lord for confirmation. He will then tell you, by your feelings, that it is right, or he will cause a stupor of thought (the absence of a confirmation, the continuation of doubt) which will tell you to start over, to re-think, to look some more."

He used the example of the brother of Jared, who got no light for his boats until he presented his own molten stones for the Lord to touch. He used the example of a wise father whose son asks him to do his math problem and who says, "No, son, you work it out, but then bring it to me and I'll tell you if you're right."

By the end of the session, Jared understood the principle. The bishop put his arm around Jared's shoulders and said, "I think *your* decision is already made, Jared. But think it through again; then fast; then go to a private place and petition the Lord for confirmation. As you do, I promise you a great spiritual experience."

Jared did so, and the bishop's promise was fulfilled. High on a mountainside he received absolute confirmation.

   He and Lydia have been married for many years now, and when there are rough spots in their relationship Jared does *not* (as do some others he knows) think to himself, "Maybe we weren't right for each other. Maybe we were too young to really know. Maybe I married the wrong person." Instead, at those rough times, Jared thinks back on the simple, sure, absolute feelings that came on the mountainside, and then, with assurance, he and Lydia work out the problem.

Postscript:

Remember
that when you take a decision to the Lord,
his promise is that you will receive *either*
a confirmation or a stupor of thought.
Both are real answers. Both require action from you.
The first should spur you toward implementation,
the second should cause you to think further or to
   look further,
or both.

When?

When Is the Right Time?

This should be the easiest question
in the book, yet
we often make it the hardest.

After the questions of *why* and *who* are answered,
the *when* should be a natural,
but we turn it into a dilemma.
We wonder about the most "convenient" time,
the most "prudent" time, the most "sensible" time.
Perhaps we wait two years for graduation
or for a better salary
or until we can own a home.
Putting off marriage (after you know the *who*)
is like postponing a trip to the moon
in order to go across the street.

The answers come as easily as the questions.
"Wouldn't we have to struggle unnecessarily if
we get married now?"
Yes! But struggling together is not unnecessary—
no matter when you marry
there will be obstacles,

there will be problems to struggle with
together.
And that's the point—
to meet life's challenges
and surmount them
together.
It really *is* necessary
because that's how an eternal marriage
is forged.

"Wouldn't it be easier on everyone
if school were finished,
or if we had a permanent home?"
Yes! But "easy" is the wrong objective.
"Wouldn't it be better for the children we'll have
if we waited until we could give them more?"
No! Because the things they need *most*
you can give them now.
"But wouldn't we be *more sure*
that we are right for each other
if we test the relationship
during a long engagement?"
Ahah! There, at last, is a valid reason for waiting.
If you are not yet sure on the *who* question,
if you don't have confirmation,
or if you feel you are not yet mature enough
to recognize the *who* answer
or to make the *who* commitment,
then, yes, it is too early even to *ask* the *when*
    question—
let alone answer it!

But again,
if the *who* is answered,
the *when* should be a matter
for only small adjustment.

If graduation is only a month or two away,
if serious financial situations can be improved
over the next several weeks,
if family matters require a short visit,
by all means, be sensible.
But long engagements for reasons of convenience
    or ease
should be rejected.
They invite problems.
They pull hard on a relationship
not yet reinforced with the steel of eternal
    commitment.

Struggling together, scrimping together,
seeking the first home or first job together —
all are great blessings,
all increase the fusing power involved
in two people becoming one.

After all, would someone delay
the starting of a *kingdom*
for any reason less important than the kingdom itself?
Marriage in the house of the Lord
is nothing less than the beginning
of a kingdom —
a kingdom within his kingdom.

In summary, there are two basic mistakes to avoid
on the *when* question.
One is trying to decide the *when*
before the *why* and *who* are absolute.
The other is considering potential long-term-delay
    factors
that are not worth the risks of waiting.

For Instance:
Struggle and Stability

Ray and Leslie got engaged in April and, after some deep soul-searching, they decided to set their temple wedding for August, just days before Ray was to start graduate school.

Some of their friends, particularly one of Leslie's uncles, advised them strongly to wait a year or two, to get the degree first—and a job—and then start the marriage with a little money in their pockets, a little stability in their lives.

They couldn't argue with his logic, but Ray and Leslie had experienced a remarkable spiritual confirmation of their love for each other, and to face the challenges of the next period of their lives separately rather than together made no sense to either of them.

Their honeymoon was the five-day drive across country to school in the old blue Ford. Leslie found a teaching job that barely covered rent and food. Ray worked at everything from apartment management to driving lessons for foreign students, in this way making enough to cover books and most of tuition. They borrowed the balance—at low, student-loan rates. Both sets of parents offered to help, but the feeling of independence and of being a new, separate family rather than an extension of two others meant too much to Ray and Leslie. Ray took to justifying the small amount they owed the bank by calling it an investment instead of a loan and by quoting Benjamin Franklin, who said, "If a man empties his purse into his head, he can never be robbed."

Just a year after their marriage—at the start of the second year of graduate school—they had their first child, a beautiful baby girl. No more income from Leslie meant more odd jobs for Ray, but they had each other, and things somehow got happier and happier in spite of the struggle.

To say it wasn't easy would be an understatement, but they thrived on it. Ray did well enough the first two terms to earn a tuition scholarship for the remainder. (He claims he made it because he *had* to — he never would have if things had been easier.)

Purely by coincidence, the only other Mormon in Ray's graduate program was a fellow named Dave who had faced a similar decision and made the opposite choice. He planned a two-year engagement, and his fiancée was working to save money for the future. On paper, Dave had it easy. His parents were paying for his schooling and living costs, and he had no family expenses to worry about.

But all Ray had to do to be sure his own decision was the right one was to be around Dave. The loneliness was only part of his problem. The bigger part was that Dave was facing challenges alone, growing from them as his fiancée was growing from her own separate challenges thousands of miles away. They were both growing, but they were growing apart — apart from each other. As it turned out, they eventually did get married, but not without several close calls and not without the loss of two years of growth *together.*

It is interesting that today, fifteen years after Ray and Leslie's decision and marriage, you can ask them to name the best experiences of their marriage and more than half of their answers will come from the "graduate school struggle period."

II
The
Right
Marriage

Where?

Where But in the Temple?

Temple marriage.
If we grow up in the Church, we grow up
with these words branded into our consciousness.
They represent almost every mother's dream for her
    daughter,
almost every father's hope for his son.
Temple marriage is too often seen as a destination
rather than a beginning,
but it is a part of our thought pattern,
a part of our view of the right life,
a part of our vision of why we are here.

We often go into it
(the temple itself as well as the temple marriage itself)
knowing not much more than that,
and not knowing — not at all —
what to expect.
Some harbor a lot of fears about what happens
in the temple,
both in the endowment and in the marriage ceremony.
Others never think about it enough to fear it.
Still others just go in with blind trust,

full of faith that whatever happens there,
understood or not understood,
will be right and good.
All three perspectives are natural — and common.
But there is a much better perspective,
a perspective of preparation and prior understanding.
The temple ceremonies are highly symbolic.
The symbols are teaching methods.
If one enters the temple with the attitude
of going to an exceptional university — the Lord's
    university —
a school which, through instruction and symbolism,
will teach him the things of eternity
(in a way that is graphic and memorable)
and which allows him both to make and to receive
    important promises —
if one enters with this attitude,
all will be well.
No one, of course, comprehends the endowment fully
upon his first temple visit
(or upon his thousandth).
So the effort should not be to grasp and learn it
all at once,
but rather to open oneself fully
to the spirit that is there,
to *feel* the beauty and take in the peace,
and then to decide to return often
so the meaning can build
and the understanding can grow.

Now, one more hard question
relating to the *where*:
Let's say we all agree that temples are beautiful,
that the words "for time and eternity"
are better than "till death do you part,"
that those in authority are wise in counseling

us not to accept less than a temple marriage.
The question still remains—
Does the mere fact that the marriage
is performed in the temple
really make it a better marriage?
in practical terms? in the day-to-day?
Does the fact that it was performed there
magically make the couples more compatible,
more considerate?
Is the husband a better husband,
the wife a better wife?
In other words, the theory and promise
of temple marriage
are wonderful,
but do they really ensure a stronger *relationship*
ten years from now?
Answer:
No, the temple ceremony won't *ensure* anything.
But the real essence of marriage
is *commitment.*
The stronger the commitment, the better the
    marriage's chance.
Eternal marriage is, by definition,
a *stronger commitment,*
and, just in that, it greatly strengthens
a marriage's chances for success.
Additionally, the spiritual nature of a temple marriage
makes it more likely that a couple
will make their partnership a three-way relationship
by including the Lord
and seeking his help in all family matters.
Taken all together—
the beauty, the commitment, the promises given and
    received—
there *is* only one place to be married.
Where but in the temple?

Indeed,
where else!

Postscript:

Have you ever thought of the many reasons for
a temple marriage?
1. It is the Lord's way.
2. It is in harmony with the sacred nature of
    marriage.
3. It improves the chances of marital happiness.
4. It provides for possible eternal association of
    husband and wife.
5. It provides for possible eternal family relationship.
6. It is a restraint against evil.
7. It is an opportunity for eternal progression.
8. It puts the family under the protection of the
    priesthood.
9. It provides a God-like destiny for human beings.
10. It is a step toward eternal increase.
11. It rules out elopements and secret marriages.
12. It provides a beautiful and ideal place for the
    marriage ceremony.
13. It provides a great ideal.
14. It provides a preparation in the priesthood and in
    character.
15. It provides counsel and cooperation with others.
16. It strengthens a common religious basis for both
    parties concerned.
17. It makes God a partner.
18. It puts the Church behind the commitment.
19. It helps guarantee activity and association in the
    Church.
20. It provides a choice person — one who is
    sympathetic, cooperative and spiritually trained
    — to perform the ceremony.

For Instance: "Twin Opposites"

Carolyn and Marilyn! "A matched pair," everyone called them: identical twins, best friends, singing duet, inseparable companions. Even in college, where so many go their separate ways, these two stayed together. As a matter of fact, they even fell in love the same year. The only thing that could have made it *more* similar would have been if their boyfriends had been brothers or twins.

As it was, the two fiancés had some major differences. Carolyn's intended, Bill, was only semi-active in the Church and was against temple marriage because his mother, who was a nonmember, would be unable to attend. He and Carolyn planned (or at least Carolyn planned and Bill nodded his head) on being sealed in the temple after a year or so.

Marilyn and Bob, on the other hand, were not only planning on the temple but doing all they could to prepare for it.

The weddings were only a month apart, and both marriages were beautiful, happy affairs. The receptions were almost identical; even the guests coming through the reception lines seemed like a re-run.

The differences started to show a year or so later. Both couples were still in school and both had some rough times financially. Relationships were strained. Levels of commitment were tested.

This may be an oversimplified analysis but *because Marilyn and Bob's commitment was longer, it was stronger*, and the difficulties that stretched it seemed to reinforce it. The same kind of rough spots in Carolyn and Bill's marriage seemed to pull their commitment until it was threadbare and weak.

A year later, Carolyn left Bill. They both claimed to love each other still, but the problems seemed bigger than the solutions — and bigger than the commitment. Bill had made little progress in the Church, and Carolyn, though still strong in her testimony, had stopped attending. Luckily (that seems a strange word to use) they had no children yet. Carolyn had often thought that if there had been a child, the commitment might have strengthened. "But the risk would have become bigger, too," she told herself.

Suddenly the twins — always so much alike before — found themselves living opposite lives.

What?

What Makes Marriage Eternal?

What is the difference, the key difference,
between temple marriage and civil marriage?
Easy! One is eternal, the other "till death";
one is long (very long), the other is short.
It's a difference of quantity — right?

No! Not right, at least, not necessarily right.
It's that kind of thinking
that gets a lot of us into serious trouble.
We think the temple is a quantity guarantee;
we think there's *more of it* when it happens there,
because it goes on forever.

But of course that forever part may or may not be true.
The *quantity* is determined by the *quality* —
the marriage will last *long* only if it lasts *well*.
There is no guarantee.
All of the promises (the unbelievable promises)
are *conditional* —
they depend on *quality*.

You might correctly say that what distinguishes
a temple marriage

and what makes it desirable above all else
is where it is performed.
But remember that *eternal marriage* is
something beyond *temple marriage.*
It goes beyond by virtue of its *quality,*
and its quality makes its quantity unmeasurable
because it is eternal.

Just as we work out our own salvation
through the quality of our individual lives,
we work out our eternal marriage
through the quality of our lives together.

You can measure the quality of your marriage
by measuring your happiness.
Just as no other success can compensate for
failure in the home,
so also can no other failure
overshadow or supersede *success* in the home
and in marriage.

Before we leave the subject of guarantees,
it should be mentioned
that there *are* guarantees,
and they can come on this earth.
All the conditional promises of the temple
can be made unconditional
by the Holy Spirit of Promise—
the assurance, the guarantee
that *can* come to the lives
and into the marriages
of those who want it badly enough
to deserve it.
Because it is a question of quality,
the *what* is really a question of *how,*

so let's concentrate for the rest of the book
on that very question —
the question of *how.*

For Instance:
Either/Or . . . or Neither

"I would say you were on the horns of the proverbial
dilemma," Susan's dad said, looking deeply into her
eyes. "And I'm not sure I know enough about either of
your options to help you very much. From what you've
told me, there's no easy answer."

It wasn't what Susan wanted to hear. It was a cool,
moonlit autumn evening, and she had just unloaded the
details of her dilemma to her father as they walked,
hand in hand, along the deserted street.

Susan's dilemma was one many girls dream of
having, but few enjoy once the moment arrives. She
had been proposed to by two boys.

One of them, Greg, was (at least on the surface)
really everything she had always told herself she
wanted in a husband: a returned missionary, quite
active in the Church, the son of a former bishop. The
other suitor, Lance, was not even a member of the
Church.

The irony was that her feelings were all backwards
from what she thought they should be. It was Lance
whom she respected most. Church member or not, he
was honest and — she searched for the right word —
noble. You could count on him; he cared for other
people. He was gentle and compassionate. In fact
(Susan surprised herself with the description) he was
Christlike in many ways. She trusted him. He had
treated her with respect, never even suggesting any-

thing wrong. And she respected him, and his ability. He
was a serious student with good grades and high ambitions.

Greg, for all his right appearances, had opposite ten-
dencies. Susan felt a certain attraction for him, but
didn't know if she trusted or respected him. It was only
her firm refusal that had kept them from going further
than they should have physically on several occasions,
and Susan sometimes had the distinct feeling that Greg
was more concerned about her feelings for him than
about his for her. He wore his Church activity a little
like a badge on his sleeve and put off some people with
his self-righteousness. His approach to life was a bit
lazy; it was hard for him to think or talk much about
ambitions or goals or life aims.

Susan's dad, after listening carefully and after
asking the questions he'd been storing up as he'd
watched the two relationships develop, didn't try to give
her an answer. But he did make points that he thought
Susan should consider:

1. Hearts are more important than badges on
sleeves. If Lance had the better heart and was the better
man, then he would likely make the better husband.

2. Good as a man is, you should never count on his
joining the Church after marriage. It can happen, and
often it does—with absolutely wonderful results. But
the odds are against it; the percentages aren't good. And
those who join the Church only in order to persuade a
girl to marry them have a slim chance of strong activity
and testimony.

Her dad held both of her hands and pulled Susan
close. "Honey, I wish I could make it easier for you. But
I think any further guidance will have to come from
your other Father. He's the one who knows. I'll pray
with you. Remember one thing, though—and I feel
strongly about this—there are not two options. There

are three. The third is that maybe neither Greg nor Lance is right — at least, not now. Perhaps in time Greg will change or Lance will convert. Or perhaps some perfect combination of Greg and Lance will come along, someone you've not yet met."

III

The
Right
Beginning

How?

How to Start Strong

How
is the *on going* question
and the one whose answer
makes the other five questions
lasting,
in both their meaning and their rewards.
Even after *why, who, when, what* and *where*
have been correctly answered
and implemented,
marriage will go no where
without the *how.*
Like a flawless ball game that is lost in the ninth
   inning
by an error,
not knowing the *how*
can cancel out right answers
on all the other questions.

And *how* is *not* a simple question.
There is no overall answer,
no panacea,
no easy formula.
But there are some guidelines,

some God-given guidelines,
that provide the framework for the *how*.
It's up to us
to build the structure of our marriage
on that framework.

The essence of this chapter
is to give direct, down-to-earth
hows
for the first six months of a brand new marriage.
As in a race,
the beginning of a marriage is often the most crucial
    part
and may determine the remainder and the result.

There are three patterns—
three channels of effort—
which are the keys to a marriage's
successful beginning.
If you can learn them,
grasp them,
implement them
during the first half-year of your marriage,
you will cut a course so deep and so correct
that it will likely guide your oneness
for the next fifty years.

The three keys are
(and be careful, because they sound easier than they
    are):
1. Continue the courtship.
2. Become (within yourself) a competent husband/
    wife.
3. Become (together) a "partnership of one."
Let's take them one at a time
and in detail,

and then look at a "for instance" that
incorporates them all.

1. *Continue the Courtship*
Contrary to what you may have heard,
chivalry and romance are not silly
or meaningless
or old-fashioned.
They are integral parts
of falling in love.
And did you know that
if you continue them,
you will continue falling in love?
(It's interesting that we usually think of falling in love
as a process that concludes, completes, finishes
at or before the wedding,
but it doesn't need to be so —
we can *keep* falling, endlessly.)

Think for a moment about the cause and effect
of courtship.
He courts her,
impresses her,
compliments her,
because he wants to *win* her.
She looks her best,
builds his ego,
does little things for him
because she wants to *win* him.
So they fall in love, win each other, get married.
End of courtship, right? End of "winning," right?
No! Not right.
The idea is to win each other *for eternity.*
That is the real prize.
And it takes a lifetime — a lifetime
of *courtship.*

Thinking this way puts everything in a new
     perspective.
The reason for courtship *was winning,*
and the reason for courtship *still is* winning.
A couple that keeps falling further in love
year after year
is heading directly toward an eternal marriage.

All right, so how do you continue a courtship?
Wait a minute.
You knew how before marriage,
and the answer is no different now.
"But we're together all the time," you say,
"we're too *used* to each other
to do those same romantic things."
No, you're not.
Just do them.
They still have the same magic.
Open doors for her,
compliment her,
pamper her a little,
take the time (daily) to think what she needs most.
Appreciate all that he does,
let him know when you are especially proud of him.
Look nice for each other,
surprise each other.

A simple device that keeps
almost all of these parts of courtship alive
is to have a weekly *date.*
Set a pattern early in your marriage of setting aside
one night of the week
to go on a full-fledged date.
"But we're together every night, anyway," you say.
A *date* is not just being together.
It is doing something special together.

A date is what it was before you were married —
going somewhere together,
treating each other in a special way,
holding hands,
saying things that convey love.
A regular "date evening" is as important
as a regular family home evening.
No matter how busy you get
or how long you live,
always save one night for your family
and another (separate) night for your spouse.
Continue the courtship
and continue the fall
into love.

2. *Become (Within Yourself) a Competent Husband/
    Wife*
(Let me word this from the husband's viewpoint, with
    the understanding that it applies equally to wives.)
You don't automatically become a good husband
at the moment of marriage
any more than a person becomes a good swimmer
the first time he is tossed into the water.

And you don't become a good husband
by changing your wife.
You become a husband
by changing what is inside of *you.*
A simple suggestion:
Take the time
(a good long Fast Sunday perhaps)
to sit down alone
and write two special and personal documents.
Entitle one of them, "What my wife *needs.*"
Make it a list.
Draw on all that you know about her.

What are her emotional needs?
her mental needs?
her physical needs?
her social needs?
her spiritual needs?
Think about your list long and hard.
Discover ways that you can meet those needs.
Then prepare a second document called,
"What I must be to her."
Again, make a list,
a list of the things she needs in *you*.
Now give some thought to what needs there are on the
  first list
that you can meet
by *becoming* the things on the second list.
Look at the lists at least once every week.
Think about them. Make some assessments and
  resolves.
(I think Sunday,
in a private "Sunday session" with yourself,
is the best time.
People often ask,
"What can we do on the Sabbath?"
"Sunday sessions" are marvelous activities.)
As you review the list,
think of ways
to *do* better on each item.
Write the ideas that come
on a calendar or in a date book.
Decide to *do* them
and decide *when* to do them.
Your second document ("What I must be to her")
can become a blueprint for the type of husband
you are becoming.
It may contain things like:
"A strong priesthood leader."

"A sensitive, attentive listener."
"A consistent 'appreciator' of her best qualities."
Always remember that this list
should spring from your first list,
the list of *her* needs.
Once the second document is complete,
you can *become* the qualities it lists
via the "as if" principle.
(Some might call this "self-programming.")
Simply remind yourself often of those qualities,
and act *as if*
you already possessed them.
If you are a jogger,
think through the list
every day
as you run.
If you don't jog regularly, rehearse the list while
    shaving,
while brushing your teeth,
while having your shower,
while doing anything that you do regularly, every day.
Think each quality through in *positive* terms —
"I *am* a strong priesthood leader."
Then illustrate the claim
by recalling to mind things you have done lately
that prove the point:
"I gave my wife a blessing when she was concerned
about her new Church position" or
"I lead our family in prayer each morning and
    evening."
Then add one clear, specific attitude or deed
(worded just as positively)
that you need to implement.
"I will study next week's Sunday School reading
    assignment by Thursday night."
Gradually and surely, you will *become*

the qualities on your list.
Gradually and surely,
you will meet your wife's needs
on a consistent and daily basis.
Gradually and surely, you will become
a *competent* husband —
one capable of beginning
and, ultimately, leading
an eternal kingdom!

3. *Become (Together) a "Partnership of One"*
An ideal partnership, in any endeavor,
is one in which two or more do better together
than the sum of what they could do separately.
Marriage can be the ultimate partnership.
It can be a three-way partnership, including God,
which makes two think as one (and eventually, as
      God)
and which produces a lifetime of joy
and opens the way to an eternity of progress.
There are four requirements for perfectable
      partnerships:
a. Clear objectives
b. Complete communication
c. Specialized responsibilities
d. Meaningful meetings
Let's look quickly *through* each one.

a. Clear objectives:
This is the easy one.
The objective is *oneness* —
to share all,
and someday to gain all.

b. Complete communication:
The old adage "Some things are better left unsaid"

has no place in a marriage that aims at oneness.
(By definition, things felt but not said by one
separate him from the other.)
Make a pact with each other
that you will share all that you feel.
Then make a pact with yourself
that all you say will be said lovingly
and understandingly.
For example, if you are irritated
by his tossing his socks on the floor,
tell him.
But do it with humor,
or sandwich it between two compliments,
or find some other way to say it without hurt.
And take time to talk.
When you spend your days separated,
take time in the evenings to bring each other up to
    date.

c. Specialized responsibilities:
Rarely do partnerships work well
if both partners try to do exactly the same things.
In business, one partner might handle production
and another, marketing.
One great fallacy of much of the women's rights
    movement
is the assumption that equality means sameness.
God has designed man and woman
with a specialized partnership in mind.
Some carry the specialization too far,
figuring that the man should be nothing but
    breadwinner,
the woman nothing but homemaker and child-raiser.
This robs both of portions of the joy
and deters good communication.

The best way to view marriage
is as two "limited partnerships."
(In business, a limited partnership is composed
of one "general partner" who takes the lead in an area
and one or more "limited partners" who often
are just as committed and have just as much at stake
but who are less involved with the day-to-day
    responsibility.)
Form *two* such limited partnerships.
Call one the "inner partnership,"
the one *inside* the home, with the wife as general
    partner.
Call the other the "outer partnership,"
the one outside the home, with the husband as
    general partner.
In each case, it is the general partner's responsibility
to keep the limited partner well informed
and to seek his input.
In each case, it is the limited partner's role
to stay informed,
to question the general partner,
to be as involved as time and circumstance allow.

d. Meaningful meetings:
Rather than a ritual,
prayer
within the partnership of marriage
should be a *meeting.*
Prior to addressing the third (directing) partner,
each general partner should give a brief report
on the partnership in his charge,
and the limited partner should ask whatever questions
and give whatever inputs are appropriate.
Through such discussions,
certain concerns will emerge
on which the directing partner's help is needed.

Thus the dialogue with that directing partner —
the prayer —
will be meaningful and specific.

For Instance:
A Day in the Life of . . .

(This may not necessarily be an ideal day in *your* life, but the principles used can be made to fit the kind of day *you* would design.)

6:30 A.M.: The alarm goes off. Jan and Phil wake up, dress in their jogging suits, and start off around the block. They have been married for five months. Both are still in school. Jan goes to school part-time and works afternoons at the hospital. Phil goes full-time (he will finish after next semester) and works three nights a week at the computer center.

They jog together, but they don't talk. The quiet early morning has become, for them, a time of introspection and thought. As they jog, each reviews mentally the "as if" principles they have developed, Phil's on "husbandship," Jan's on "wifeship." As Phil runs, he is thinking, "I am sensitive to Jan and appreciative of her." He has five qualities which he reviews and in terms of which he thinks about recent things he has done that illustrate that he *is* those qualities.

Their morning prayer is a kneeling one, after they finish their run. They find that they are more alert and pray with more concentration this way than when they roll right out of bed and onto their knees.

Phil walks into the bathroom to shave and sees Jan's handwriting on the mirror, in lipstick: "I love you." He smiles, reaches out to wipe it off, thinks better of it, and shaves looking through and between the red marks.

Phil has an early class and has to leave first. As he kisses Jan good-bye, he slips a note into her hand.

12:10 P.M.: Jan comes out of her class and waits by the curb. She opens Phil's note and reads it again: "Honey, it's not in lipstick, but I love you, too. I'll pick you up after your class for a surprise."

The surprise turns out to be a picnic. Phil has been by the gourmet section of the supermarket and has a loaf of French bread, some Dutch Havarti cheese, and a bottle of nonalcoholic sparkling grape juice. He pulls up to the curb, runs around to open her door, and whisks her off to a grassy hill at the remote part of the campus. He spreads out a green and white checkered tablecloth (the same one they used for picnics before they were married).

11:00 P.M.: On their knees, ready to retire, Jan and Phil hold their nightly partnership meeting. Phil reviews his day, and as he talks about two job interviews he has lined up, a short discussion ensues about the pros and cons of taking a job in a large east coast city. Jan mentions a difficult assignment in her English literature class and then asks Phil's feelings about some wallpaper samples she has been considering for the apartment's kitchen. They laugh for a moment as they project how much different Jan's "inner partnership" report will be when there are children to be reported on. They discuss again their desire for a first child and recall the strong confirmation of that decision that they experienced the Fast Sunday before.

Their prayer reflects the needs and gratitude connected with the things they have just discussed. Their verbal prayer is a shared one. Jan starts and, when she has finished, rather than closing the prayer, simply squeezes Phil's hand and he continues with what he wishes to say. Then he closes for both of them in the name of Jesus Christ.

IV

The
Right
Result

How?
(Continued)

How to Keep It Working

Let's say you've just read the preceding story
(Jan and Phil, newlyweds, in an idyllic existence)
and let's say that sort of thing is
ten or twenty years behind you now.
Let's say that as you read it you were thinking,
"Oh, sure. That sort of stuff would work *really* well
    now—
with our five children
and two dogs
and big mortgage
and fifty or a hundred other pressures."
(I'll forgive you for a little sarcasm.)

The question is, of course,
Can it still work?
Or you might even start with a more basic question:
Does it still need to work?
"After all," you may reason, "we're committed to each
    other,
we've been married a long time,
we're used to each other.
There's no time now for that romance

and planning and self-improvement and one-on-one
   communication.
Maybe in another decade or two,
when the children are raised and gone—
maybe then we can get back to
that sort of thing."
That is the kind of thinking
that charts a direction of doom
for a marriage.
Love and marriage are never static.
You are always falling a little more *in*
or a little more *out.*

How does one make certain that it's more *in* and not
   more *out?*
First of all, realize that the three keys
offered in the last chapter
(courtship, inner self-improvement, partnership)
are *more* (not less) important now.
Second, realize that you *can*
still implement all three
despite the kids and the dogs and the mortgage.
You *can* still have the "partnership meetings"
before retiring each night.
You *can* still think through the kind of husband
or wife you are striving to be—
while running, while shaving, while feeding those dogs,
while doing anything you do every day.
And you *can* continue the courtship,
because courtship, more than anything,
is a state of mind.

Now, let's say that you feel
your marriage is not yet perfect
(that should allow everyone to read on)
and let's say that, as you think about it,

you decide it's about time to rejuvenate it,
to revitalize it to some degree.
Here is a suggestion:
Have a second honeymoon—
and use it not only to be alone together,
but to lay your own specific goals and plans
for the next five years of your marriage.
For starters, don't feel guilty
about leaving the children,
as long as they are well cared for
by grandparents
or a young "housesitting" couple who will stay in
    your own home,
or whatever you can arrange that is secure.
It is very likely good for the children
as well as good for you,
to be separated occasionally.
It is especially good for them
if you are using the time
to improve your marriage.

You will know much more specifically
than anyone else
what things your marriage needs.
But the following list may prompt some thought
and suggest some areas of discussion.
Wherever you go for "Honeymoon II,"
take some notepaper.
Plan to return with a written five-year plan.

Here are some suggestions for your format:
1. Start with the positive.
Take some time to remember the best times,
to count your blessings,
to realize all you have now that you didn't have then.
Have a "gratitude prayer" and thank the Lord for it all.

2. Then get serious and specific about problems.
First list the *external* problems
that have some effect on your marriage:
finances,
work difficulties,
relationships with other people,
and so on.
Then focus on *internal* problems:
communication,
differences in aspirations and goals,
discipline of children,
and so on again.

Do this *early* in "Honeymoon II,"
and say *all* that you feel —
with the reassurance that much time remains
to resolve the differences
and to come together on the divisions.

3. Use prayer and scripture to set the spirit and tone
for each day and each discussion.
Perhaps you should bring *only* your notepaper
and your scriptures —
nothing else to distract or diffuse.

4. Have a private testimony meeting
at least once during the first or second day.
In a more formal way, and closing in Jesus Christ's
     name,
express your deepest feelings and beliefs
to each other.

5. Where possible, develop straightforward solutions
for both the external and internal problems
you uncover.

Where solutions are beyond your control (in the
   external),
discuss how to live with the problem
and resolve to continue its discussion
and to make the best of it.

6. Formulate five-year goals
for both the inner and the outer partnership (see
   previous chapter).
Close your eyes and use your imaginations—
try to describe your family and home five years from
   now.
Do the same with your profession and with your
   Church activity.
Describe the ideal in each case
and then try to develop goals that can make ideals
into reality.

7. Resolve to take a mini-honeymoon each year
(at least a day and a night away—together).
The best time may be near the new year
when yearly goals
can be broken out of the five-year framework.
But any time of year will work—as long as you
do it
every year.

8. Begin the process of having a weekly
"executive session"
following or preceding family home meeting on
   Sunday.
Find a regular time on Sunday
(and it may have to be very early or quite late)
when just the two of you
can review the week behind
and look to the week ahead—

with regard to short-term goals.
Think in monthly terms
during the executive session that falls on Fast Sunday.

9. Add one further element to the nightly
    "partnership meetings"
discussed in the previous chapter.
Develop a simple, one-page form
with the hours of the day listed down the left-hand
    margin
and a heavy dividing line running vertically down the
    center.
Keep a stack of them on a clipboard — with carbon
    paper.
Each night,
after the brief partnership reports
and before the prayer,
plan your respective days together —
his in one column, hers parallel in the other column.
Each one keeps a copy during the following day.
Knowing what the other partner is doing
(as well as knowing more precisely what *you* are doing)
will help your partnership in several ways.

10. Resolve together (and individually)
to try to "out-give" each other.
Any marriage team
on which each player
decides he will give fifty percent —
not one bit more —
will fail.
Decide to *give eighty* or *ninety* percent.
Create "giving overlap"
and things that were once problems
will become blessings.

11. Learn to use a *listening* technique.
Some marriages have bad communication
because the partners don't talk,
they don't say all that they feel.
Others have bad communication
because the partners don't *listen.*
Listening is an *art*, a skill, a talent to be developed.
A useful technique is that called Rogerian
(after noted psychiatrist Karl Rogers).
It consists of repeating back (in different words)
what you hear the other person saying.
You do not direct the conversation in any way,
or even throw any new elements into it.
Simply listen, rephrase, and report.
For example:
She says, "Whew, it's good to have you home. It's
  been a bad day!"
He says, "You've had a tough day."
She: "Well, a long one at least.
Susan fell on her bike
and the visiting teachers stayed for two hours."
He: "Susan fell, and the sisters were here that long?"
She: "Yes, but Sue is okay. Dinner isn't even ready yet.
I've had a hard time concentrating on anything today."
He: "You've had a lot on your mind, I guess, dear,
and it's not easy."
She: "You know what I think it is?
It's that new PTA responsibility.
I know nothing about it
and I think I'm more worried about it than I realize."

The simple fact is that
people will get to the heart of their feelings
more quickly when they are being *listened* to
than when they are being directed.

The "Honeymoon II" format for discussion
outlined above
is hard work,
and it may not sound very appealing at first.
But remember that marriage requires hard mental
    work,
and it is worth every bit of it.
And something else:
The best times, the most fun, the deepest relaxation
all seem to *follow* hard mental effort.
Perhaps by making it a *working* vacation
you will make "Honeymoon II"
the most relaxing and refreshing moment
of your marriage thus far.

A point to remember:
If the above doesn't seem to apply
to your situation,
or if you do not have partner cooperation,
do the things you can alone.

For Instance:
Faded Joys Recalled

"The idealism of youth," Bill thought as he closed
his old diary.

The little volume was fourteen years old now, and it
covered the period of his engagement and marriage to
Paula. It talked about their communication, their goals,
their commitments to stay as much in love as they were
then. While thumbing through it, Bill recalled for the
first time in years how they used to take a walk every
Sunday, winter or summer, in the little park by their
apartment, discussing their future life, sharing their
individual concerns, planning the coming week. The